CAMBRIDGE

Pre A1 Starters 4

AUTHENTIC PRACTICE TESTS

STUDENT'S BOOK
WITHOUT ANSWERS
WITH AUDIO

Cambridge University Press
www.cambridge.org/elt

Cambridge Assessment English
www.cambridgeenglish.org

Information on this title: www.cambridge.org/9781009036238

First published 2022

20 19 18 17 16 15 14 13

Printed in Brazil by Forma Certa Grafica Digital LTDA

A catalogue record for this publication is available from the British Library

ISBN 978-1-009-03626-9 Student's Book with Answers with Audio with Resource Bank
ISBN 978-1-009-03623-8 Student's Book without Answers with Audio

The authors and publishers acknowledge the following sources of copyright material and are grateful for the permissions granted. While every effort has been made, it has not always been possible to identify the sources of all the material used, or to trace all copyright holders. If any omissions are brought to our notice, we will be happy to include the appropriate acknowledgements on reprinting and in the next update to the digital edition, as applicable.

Illustrations: Cambridge Assessment

Audio production by dsound recording studios

Typeset by QBS Learning

Cover illustration: Leo Trinidad/Astound

Contents

Part 1

– 5 questions –

Listening test audio

Listen and draw lines. There is one example.

Sue Mark Alice Hugo

Eva Sam Ben

Part 2

– 5 questions –

Listening test audio

Read the question. Listen and write a name or a number. There are two examples.

Examples

What is the teacher's name? Mrs ....Pen........

How old is Alex? ....8........

Questions

1 What is Alex's family name? ....

2 Where does Alex live? .... Street

3 Which number is Alex's house? ....

4 What is Alex's sister's name? ....

5 How many children are in the football class? ....

Part 3

– 5 questions –

Listening test audio

Listen and tick (✔) the box.
There is one example.

Which is the boy's lunch?

A ✔ B ☐ C ☐

1 Which is Dan's new T-shirt?

A ☐ B ☐ C ☐

2 Where does the girl's grandma live?

A ☐ B ☐ C ☐

3 Where is Dad now?

A ☐ **B** ☐ **C** ☐

4 What is the boy's favourite animal at the zoo?

A ☐ **B** ☐ **C** ☐

5 Who is playing table tennis now?

A ☐ **B** ☐ **C** ☐

Part 4

– 5 questions –

Listen and colour. There is one example.

Part 1

– 5 questions –

Look and read. Put a tick (✔) or a cross (✘) in the box.
There are two examples.

Examples

This is a watch. ✔

These are motorbikes. ✘

Questions

1

This is a board. ☐

2

These are shorts. ☐

3

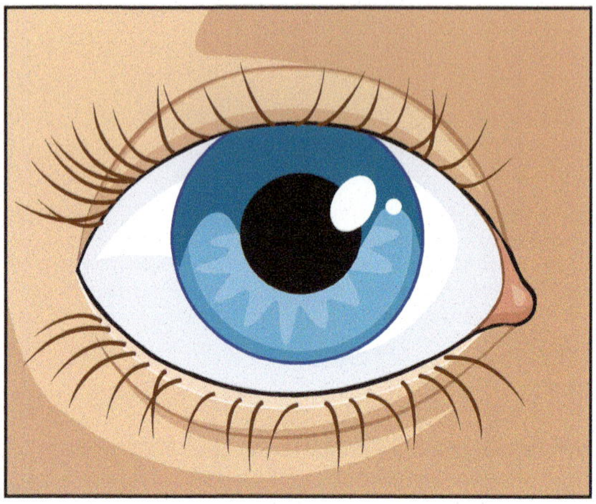

This is an ear. ☐

4

These are limes. ☐

5

This is a tennis racket. ☐

Part 2

– 5 questions –

Look and read. Write yes or no.

Examples

The monkey is on the zebra's head. ....yes..........

The giraffe is playing the guitar. ....no..........

Questions

1 The crocodile has got a cake on its tail. ....

2 The elephant is holding four balloons. ....

3 There is a spider on the tree. ....

4 The bird has got a flower in its mouth. ....

5 The watermelon is between the bananas and the pineapple. ....

Part 3

– 5 questions –

Look at the pictures. Look at the letters. Write the words.

Example

b u s

Questions

1

_ _ _ _

2

_ _ _ _

3

_ _ _ _ _

4

_ _ _ _ _

5

_ _ _ _ _ _ _ _ _ _

Part 4

– 5 questions –

Read this. Choose a word from the box. Write the correct word next to numbers 1–5. There is one example.

Lucy's bedroom

This is Lucy's bedroom. There is a ....*table*.......... with a lamp on it and she's got a **(1)** .... for her clothes. Lucy has got some cool **(2)** .... on the walls. Lucy sits on her bed and plays **(3)** .... on her tablet. Lucy likes to listen to music on the **(4)** .... and draw pictures in her room. In the evening, she reads a **(5)** .... in bed.

Example

table

onions

book

games

radio

cupboard

baby

posters

Part 5

– 5 questions –

Look at the pictures and read the questions. Write one-word answers.

Examples

Where is the cat? on the ....keyboard........

How many children are there? ....two........

Questions

1 Who is pointing at the ball? the ....

3 What animals can Ben see at the zoo today?

A ☐

B ☐

C ☐

4 What is Dan's mum doing?

A ☐

B ☐

C ☐

5 How can Eva go to school today?

A ☐

B ☐

C ☐

Part 4

– 5 questions –

Listening test audio

Listen and colour. There is one example.

Part 1

– 5 questions –

Look and read. Put a tick (✔) or a cross (✘) in the box.
There are two examples.

Examples

This is a duck. ✔

These are rulers. ✘

Questions

1

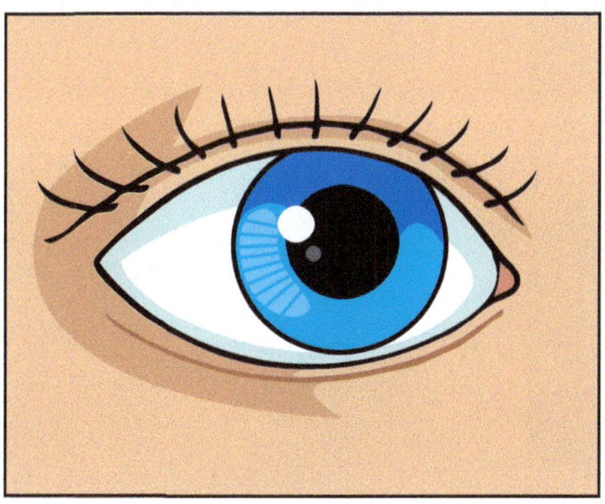

This is a nose. ☐

2

These are balloons. ☐

3

These are chairs. ☐

4

This is a jacket. ☐

5

This is a plane. ☐

Part 2

– 5 questions –

Look and read. Write yes or no.

Examples

The girl is playing the guitar. ....yes..........

The people are in the garden. ....no..........

Questions

1 The man has got a book. ....

2 There are five flowers on the table. ....

3 The baby is sleeping on the sofa. ....

4 The cat is on the rug. ....

5 The clock is between the window and the mirror. ....

Part 3

– 5 questions –

Look at the pictures. Look at the letters. Write the words.

Example

b e a n

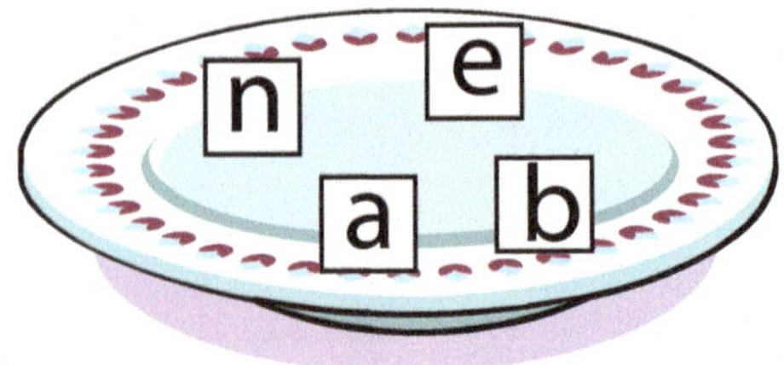

Questions

1

_ _ _ _ _

2

_ _ _ _ _

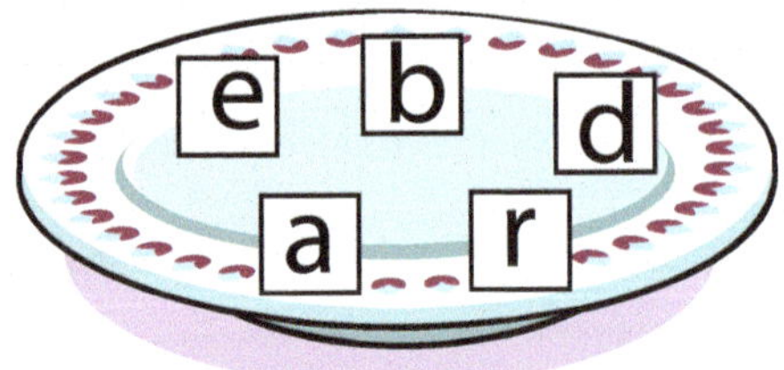

3

_ _ _ _ _ _

4

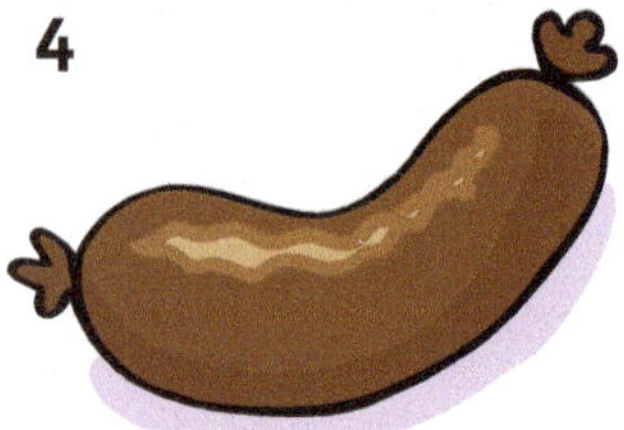

_ _ _ _ _ _ _ _

5

_ _ _ _ _ _ _ _ _ _

Part 4

– 5 questions –

Read this. Choose a word from the box. Write the correct word next to numbers 1–5. There is one example.

My cousin Nick

This is my cousin Nick. Nick lives in my street with his mum, dad and two ....brothers.... . He likes to wear T-shirts and **(1)** .... We like to go to the **(2)** .... on our bikes. Then, we get **(3)** .... – chocolate is our favourite! In the evening, we watch **(4)** .... or talk to our friends on the computer. Nick likes playing the **(5)** .... too. We love music.

Example

brothers

pear

piano

jeans

television

playground

helicopter

ice creams

Part 5

– 5 questions –

Look at the pictures and read the questions. Write one-word answers.

Examples

Where are the children? in the ......park......

What game are three of the children playing? ......tennis......

Questions

1 What have the children got on their heads? baseball ....

2 What is the boy standing on? a ....

3 What is in the boy's hand? the ....

4 How many children are playing tennis now? ....

5 Where is the boy's bag now? under the ....

Blank Page

Part 1

– 5 questions –

Listening test audio

Listen and draw lines. There is one example.

Lucy Pat Alice Tom

Grace Ben Eva

Part 2

– 5 questions –

Listening test audio

Read the question. Listen and write a name or a number. There are two examples.

Examples

What is the boy's name? ....Hugo........

How old is the boy? ....9........

Questions

1 What is Hugo's family name? ....

2 Where does Hugo live? in .... Street

3 What is the number of Hugo's house? ....

4 What is the name of Hugo's friend? ....

5 How old is Hugo's friend? ....

Part 3

– 5 questions –

Listening test audio

Listen and tick (✔) the box.
There is one example.

What does Sue want for lunch?

A ☐

B ☐

C ✔

1 Where are Mark's football boots?

A ☐

B ☐

C ☐

2 What animals are the children learning about today?

A ☐

B ☐

C ☐

3 Which is Dan's bike?

A ☐

B ☐

C ☐

4 Who is in the photo?

A ☐

B ☐

C ☐

5 What has the dog got in its mouth?

A ☐

B ☐

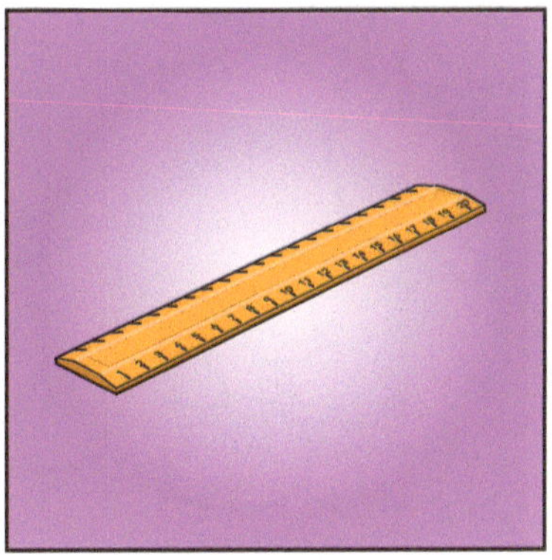

C ☐

Part 4

– 5 questions –

Listening test audio

Listen and colour. There is one example.

Part 1

– 5 questions –

Look and read. Put a tick (✓) or a cross (✗) in the box.
There are two examples.

Examples

This is a tree. ✓

These are desks. ✗

Questions

1

This is a skirt. ☐

2

This is a coconut. ☐

3

These are bees. ☐

4

These are shells. ☐

5

This is a board. ☐

Part 2

– 5 questions –

Look and read. Write yes or no.

Examples

The family is listening to music on the radio. ....yes............

The people are in the living room. ....no............

Questions

1 The family is cleaning the kitchen. ....

2 The dog is under the table. ....

3 Dad is taking a photo. ....

4 There is some food on the table. ....

5 The door is open. ....

Part 3

– 5 questions –

Look at the pictures. Look at the letters. Write the words.

Example

k i t e

Questions

1

_ _ _ _

2

_ _ _ _ _

3

_ _ _ _ _

4

_ _ _ _ _

5

_ _ _ _ _ _ _ _ _ _

Part 4

– 5 questions –

Read this. Choose a word from the box. Write the correct word next to numbers 1–5. There is one example.

Ben's pet

Ben has two pets, a ....cat........ and a mouse. The mouse's name is Kiwi. Kiwi lives in Ben's **(1)** ....

Kiwi has a brown body and very small **(2)** .... Its tail and nose are pink. Kiwi likes drinking **(3)** .... and eating fruit. Its favourite fruit is **(4)** ....

Kiwi sleeps in the day and plays at **(5)** ....

Example

cat

pencils

feet

apples

night

football

water

garden

Part 5

– 5 questions –

Look at the pictures and read the questions. Write one-word answers.

Examples

Where are the people? at the ......zoo......

Who is sitting on the green seat? ......Mum......

Questions

1 Where is one of the ice creams? on the ....

2 How many monkeys are there? ....

3 Who is pointing at the black monkey? the ....

4 What is the girl giving to her brother? a ....

5 What is the black monkey doing? ....

Blank Page

SCENE PICTURE

Blank Page

OBJECT CARDS

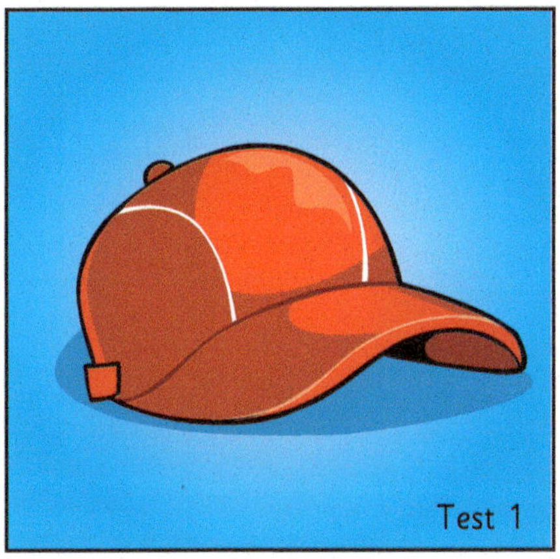

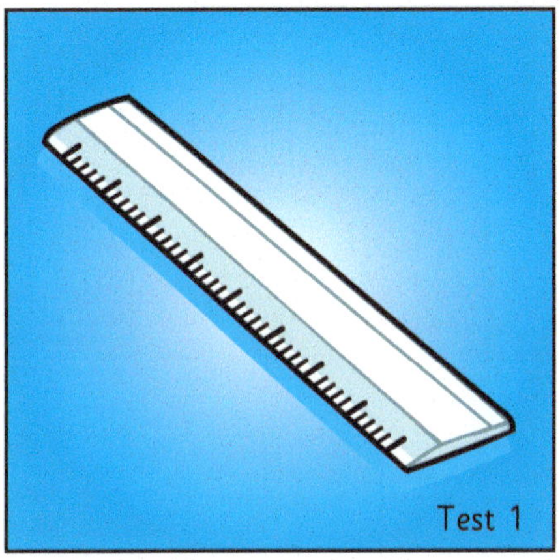

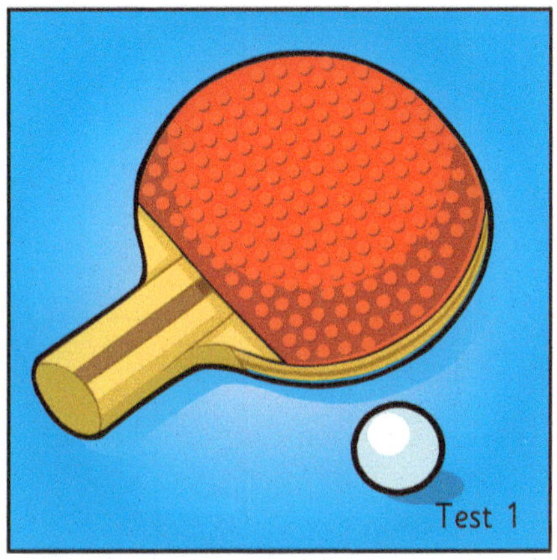

Blank Page

SCENE PICTURE

Blank Page

OBJECT CARDS

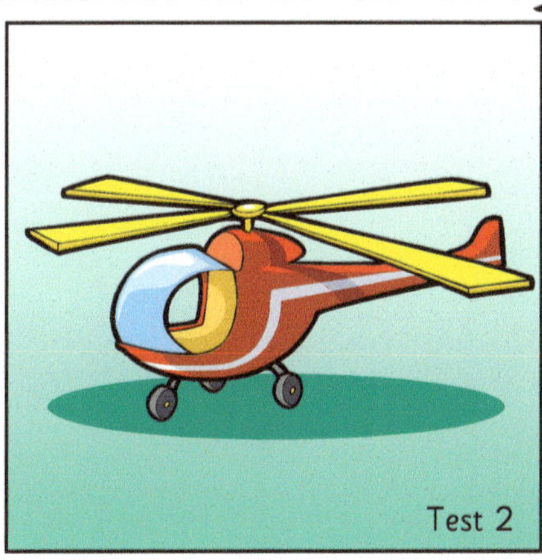

Blank Page

SCENE PICTURE

Blank Page

OBJECT CARDS

Test 3

Test 3

Test 3

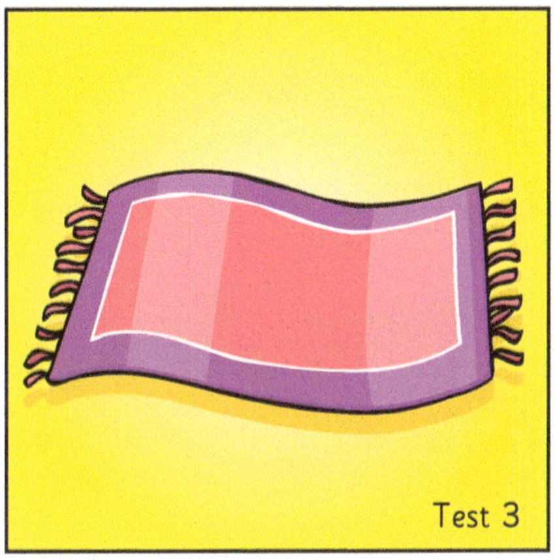
Test 3

Test 3

Test 3

Test 3

Test 3

Blank Page